COTSWOLD

A PICTORIAL CELEBRATION

Sketchbook

Jim Watson

Window at Upper Oddington

SURVIVAL BOOKS • LONDON • ENGLAND

Jewellery shop at Stow-on-the-Wold

First published 2010

Text, illustrations and maps © Jim Watson 2010

Survival Books Limited
9 Bentinck Street, London, W1U 2EL, United Kingdom
Tel: +44 (0)20-7788 7644. Fax: +44 (0)870-762 3212
email: info@survivalbooks.net
website: www.survivalbooks.net

British Library Cataloguing in Publication Data
ACIP record for this book is available
from the British Library.
ISBN: 978-1-907339-10-3

Front cover illustration: Guiting Power

Printed and bound in India by Ajanta Offset

CONTENTS

Fox on the thatch at Stanton

3

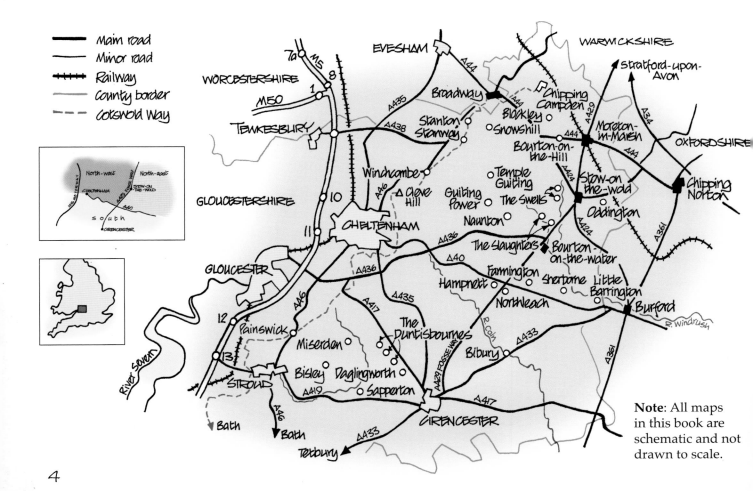

Note: All maps in this book are schematic and not drawn to scale.

4

INTRODUCTION

The Cotswolds are unique, a timeless landscape of tranquil country lanes, rolling hills and deep wooded valleys. But it's to the small towns and villages that our attention always returns. Places of warm, honey-coloured stone, steeped in history and an undefinable 'Englishness' that makes you immediately feel at home.

The region has been the favourite haunt of royalty and the landed gentry for centuries and now also of latterday show-biz 'celebrities' and rock stars. Those of us who live in urban areas see it as an litter-free country idyll, without graffiti, CCTV cameras, fast food outlets or sprawling industrial estates. Given a big National Lottery win, we could also live in a place like that.

This book is a collection of my favourite Cotswold places. It's a personal choice, enabled by the region having no precise boundaries. There are those who argue that it extends as far south as Bath, but for me the essence of the Cotswolds is concentrated most richly within the county of Gloucestershire. The notes accompanying the illustrations provide some historical background and useful facts and figures.

This is prime walking country. The superb Cotswold Way long-distance footpath crosses the region and there's a multitude of books and web pages covering other routes.

I hope this book will guide you to some of my favourite places in the Cotswolds and that they give you as much pleasure as they do me whenever I visit.

Jim Watson

Rugby, 2010

Hampnett

5

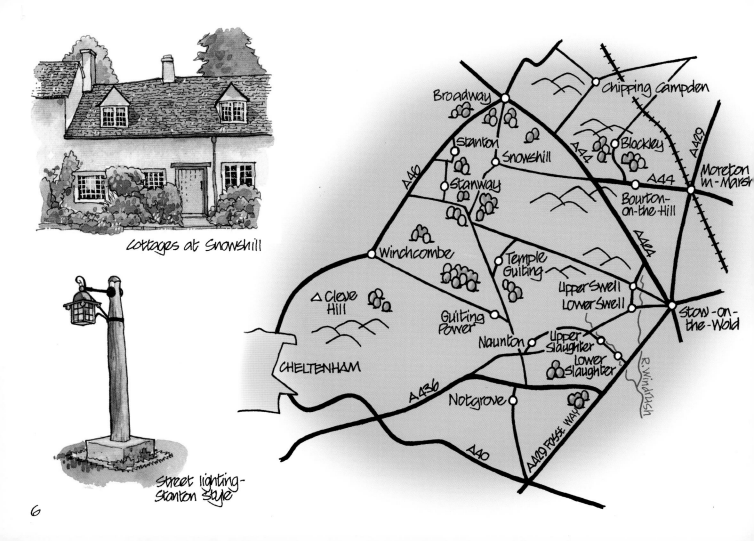

Cottages at Snowshill

Street lighting - Stanton Style

Broadway

Stanton

Snowshill

Stanway

Winchcombe

△ Cleve Hill

Temple Guiting

Guiting Power

CHELTENHAM

Naunton

Upper Slaughter

Lower Slaughter

Notgrove

Chipping Campden

Blockley

Moreton in-Marsh

Bourton-on-the-Hill

Upper Swell

Lower Swell

Stow-on-the-Wold

R. Windrush

A40

A44

A429

A44

A424

A436

A40

A429 FOSSE WAY

THE NORTH-WEST

It's invidious to compile a league of 'Best of the Cotswolds', but places in the North West would come high in my table.

Bordering the area are the four main towns of Broadway, Moreton-in-Marsh, Stow-on-the-Wold and Winchcombe. They're all different, yet each blessed with their own version of 'Cotswoldness'. Moreton and Stow, still the busy traveller's stops on the Fosse Way; stately Broadway; and Winchcombe, the Saxon capital of Mercia.

The villages are no less impressive: the architectural gem of Chipping Campden; the set-piece Slaughters; and the blessed trio of Cotswold perfection, Snowshill, Stanton and Stanway. For contrast, there are the smaller villages of Naunton, Notgrove, Bourton-on-the-Hill, the Guitings and the Swells, less visited but still worthwhile seeking out.

There's also dear old Blockley, rather isolated and often overlooked, but a handsome village, full of interest and with a real sense of community. It's one of my favourites.

The Cotswold escarpment is at its highest along the western side of the area providing some terrific views. Cleve Hill, south of Winchcombe, is the highest point in the Cotswolds at 1,082ft (330m) above sea level.

Cotswold stone quarried in the north is a deep golden colour due to iron deposits in the stone, and noticeably darker and warmer than stone from the south.

Overlooking Guiting Power

7

The church has a Norman chancel, with a Gothic tower added around 1725 by local quarry-owner, Thomas Woodward. The medieval bishops of Worcester made Blockley their summer residence.

Church of St Peter & St Paul

BLOCKLEY
3 miles north-west of Moreton-in-Marsh

Owned by the bishops of Worcester and administration centre of Worcestershire for 1,000 years, Blockley was transferred to Gloucester in 1931, when many county borders were revised.

It's a large village, full of character, with terraces of cottages strung across steep hillsides and ashlar stone buildings stacked above the Blockley Brook, a tributary of the River Stour.

The village post office closed in 2007, but a year later the villagers opened their own not-for-profit store, off-licence, post office and cafe in Blockley's historic Old Coach House. The Co-operative Association now has over 530 members and employs a manager and 14 part-time staff.

Bell Bank – yet another hill!

Village Shop & Cafe

The Crown Inn

One of Blockley's few flat areas

The bowling green

High Street

A fine terrace of mainly 18th and early 19th century houses. There was once 20 shops in this quiet street and the village had eight pubs.

BLOCKLEY DOORWAYS

Blockley enjoyed a short but lucrative silk boom in the early 1800s. The Rushout family, from nearby Northwick Park, established the industry and by 1823, the village had eight silk mills supplying the Coventry ribbon trade and providing employment for some 3,000 people, not only in the mills but also for families of out-workers in the surrounding farms and cottages. But, in 1860, restrictions on imported silk were removed and many of the Coventry weavers were ruined. By 1880, the Blockley mills were deserted.

Thankfully, many have now been converted to desirable homes along the river which harmonise well with the rest of this most attractive village.

Blockley has two pubs, The Crown Inn and The Great Western Arms, and you can usually park at the roadside near the shop. It's also a good centre for walks; one over Blockley Downs to Batsford Park and a steeper route up to Upton Wold. The village is also best explored on foot — but you do have to like hills!

BOURTON-ON-THE-HILL

2 miles west of Moreton-in-Marsh

Once owned by the abbots of Westminster, who kept large flocks of sheep on the nearby Bourton Downs where race horses are now trained, Bourton-on-the-Hill developed in the 17th century on a steep hill, once part of the turnpiked London, Oxford and Worcester 'Great Road', and now the busy A44.

Main Street

House on the hill

St Lawrence's church

The village has many attractive houses, including the Old School, The Retreat almshouses, and The Bank. The prosperity of the 15th century wool industry paid for a fine clerestory window in the church, which conserves a bell-metal bushel and peck from 1816, the standard measures for the collection of tithes.

Parking is possible with consideration in the streets off the Main Street. Apart from the 18th century Horse and Groom, a welcome refreshment stop at the top of the hill, the village has no facilities.

The Horse & Groom

BROADWAY
9 miles north-west of Stow-on-the-Wold

The great Cotswold showpiece village, Broadway has a wide main street edged with trim greens and a series of old stone 17th and 18th buildings, now housing a variety of gift shops, tea rooms, art galleries and antique dealers. Overlooked by the steep and wooded Cotswold edge and the stone folly of Broadway Tower, the village has something for everyone.

Situated on the main route between Oxford and Worcester, Broadway developed with the stagecoach trade and at one time had 23 inns, with seven coaches passing through every day. These days many more coaches call, but now they're luxury tourers bringing visitors from all over the world.

High Street - the 'broad way'

Part of the Lygon Arms

The great bulk of Tudor House at the east end of the High Street dates back to 1659 and now houses an antique shop. The former St Michael's Church School is dated 1856 and the projecting clock 1887. The school is now an art gallery.

The Lygon Arms, which dominates the western end of the High Street, was originally bought from General Lygon, who fought at Waterloo, by his butler, but it was developed into the world-renowned hotel of today by Sydney Bolton Russell.

Both King Charles and Oliver Cromwell are alleged to have stayed in the village – though at different times.

The former St Michael's Church School & Tudor House

15

One of the many art galleries

The village deli

Said to have been 'discovered' by William Morris, the champion of the English Arts and Crafts movement and the intellectuals of the 1890s, the popularity of Broadway grew rapidly. But, despite the pressures of mass tourism, the village remains more or less unspoilt and a walk up one side of the High Street and down the other can be an excellent way to pass a quiet afternoon.

BROADWAY TOWER

Built in 1799 by the Earl of Coventry as a focal point from his home, Croome Court in Worcestershire, about 15 miles to the north-west, Broadway Tower is a familiar landmark on the 1,024ft high Broadway Hill above the village.

The 55ft high, mock-castle folly is one of England's finest viewpoints from where you can see 14 counties, which include the Vales of Evesham and Gloucester and, on a clear day, the Welsh mountains.

Nearby, there's a memorial to the crew of an A.W.38 Whitley bomber which crashed during a training mission in June 1943.

The Tower is the central feature of a country park with a 19th century exhibition barn, car park, shop, restaurant and a woodland nature walk.

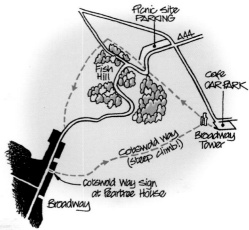

Gargoyles!

Broadway Tower

The best way to appreciate this area and its remarkable views is on a circular three mile-long walk. There's an alternative car park at a picnic site at the top of Fish Hill, from where you should follow the 'Woodland Walk' sign to cross a minor road and descend Fish Hill to join Broadway High Street at Pike Cottage.

The climb up to the Tower is steep and strenuous but the route across the hilltop is much easier. Take care crossing the busy A44.

CHIPPING CAMPDEN

5 miles north-west of Moreton-in-Marsh

The finest of all the Cotswold wool towns, dating back to the 12th century when it was on an important trading route. During the late Middle Ages, Cotswold wool became famous throughout Western Europe.

Apart from the inevitable parked cars, everything in Campden's elegant High Street is worth looking at. Many of the fine houses date from the 14th century and their honey-coloured stone still retains the glow of prosperity and well-being.

There's parking in the Square or at the roadsides.

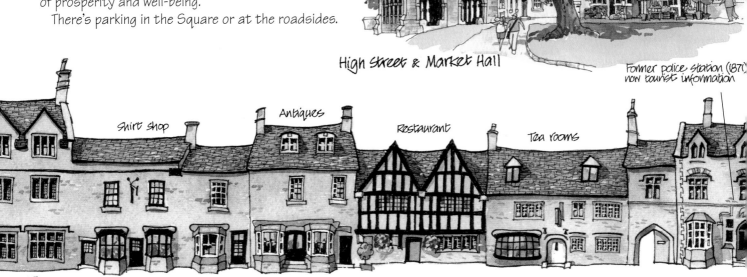

High Street & Market Hall

Former police station (1871) now tourist information

Shirt Shop

Antiques

Restaurant

Tea rooms

18

Grevel House   **Sundial**   **Gargoyles**

North-west side of High Street

Substantial buildings line both sides of the mile-long High Street in unbroken terraces. Each has its own distinct design but is also part of the wondrous whole.

The Campden Trust, founded in 1927 to preserve the town's 'unspoilt' appearance, keeps a vigilant eye on all development. There's even an unobtrusive Co-operative store on the High Street. Proof that a high profile retailer can still prosper without a garish, corporate shop front.

William Grevel, a wealthy wool merchant who died in 1401, built Grevel House as his home around 1380. The Woolstaplers Hall across the road was built a few years earlier by a wool-trader, Robert Calf, as a place for merchants to gather and buy staples of Cotswold wool.

Tea rooms   **Co-op store**   **Post Office**   **Former carriage entrance**   **Noel Arms Hotel**

South-east side of High street

Campden's Town Hall occupies an island site on the edge of a small square at the west end of the High Street. It's of uncertain age but parts date back to the 14th century. The building incorporates two buttresses, the only remaining parts of St Katherine's Chapel, built in 1180. One of the curios inside is the last surviving truncheon which special constables used against Isambard Kingdom Brunel and his engineers who wanted to bring the new railway into Campden. After fierce opposition the branch line from Stratford-on-Avon was rerouted via Honeybourne.

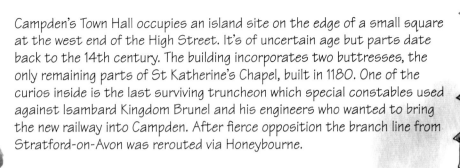

One of Campden's beautiful wrought-iron street signs

The Market Hall – also known as 'The Wool Market' – was a gift to the town by Sir Baptist Hicks in 1627 as a shelter for stalls selling butter, cheese and poultry. Hicks, a wealthy textile merchant, also represented Tavistock and Tewkesbury in the House of Commons, and in 1626 was made Viscount Campden.

A sensitively designed bus shelter!

The Market Hall

The Town Hall

There was a Norman church on the present site before 1180 but it took another 300 years before the building began to look anything like it does today. The nave was reconstructed about 1490 and the huge west tower was added around 1500. A 15th century brass commemorates William Grevel, 'flower of the wool merchants of all England'. The town's other great benefactor, Sir Baptist Hicks, who donated the pulpit and lectern, is grandly interred in the Earl of Gainsborough's family chapel.

Architectural curios abound

Hicks, a prominent Royalist, built fabulous Campden Manor next to the church in 1613. It was deliberately burnt down during the Civil War (1641-51) to prevent it falling into the hands of Oliver Cromwell's Parliamentarians. Jacobean lodges and an imposing gateway are all that remains. Hicks also built the terrace of almshouses opposite the gatehouse, which cost £1,000 in 1612 and are still in use today.

The magnificent 120ft (36m) high tower of St James' church

Campden Manor gatehouse

GUITING POWER *5 miles south-east of Winchcombe*

Situated on the slopes of a small valley formed by a tributary of the River Windrush, Guiting Power is unusual for its size in having a post office, village hall, children's nursery, bakery and two public houses; The Farmer's Arms and The Hollow Bottom. Parking is possible around the picturesque village green where restored Cotswold houses face a 1918 War Memorial Cross of medieval design. There are popular walks along the narrow and winding Windrush Valley, south to Naunton or north to Temple Guiting, or into Guiting Woods.

To a large extent, the village owes its preservation to the Guiting Manor Amenity Trust, founded by the Lord of the Manor, Raymond Cochrane, in the early 1970s as protection from the invasion of weekend second-home buyers. The Trust owns more than a hundred houses in the village, which are only rented to young people brought up in the countryside and who wish to remain there after marriage.

Church Street

The Green & War memorial

TEMPLE GUITING

2 miles north of Guiting Power

This is a scattered and rather secretive village situated in a wooded valley along the infant River Windrush. There are deep pools above and below a small bridge over the river.

Temple Guiting is an ancient site, owned by the Knights Templars around 1150 when they worked a fulling mill at nearby Barton. The village name has extended their influence over the centuries.

The Plough Inn, at the east end of the village, was voted 'Racing pub of the Year' in 2008, and has rooms overlooking the gallops of Jonjo O'Neil's training yard.

Village shop

A Cotswold doorway

MORETON-IN-MARSH

4 miles north of Stow-on-the-Wold

A busy cross-roads on the Roman Fosse Way, now the A429, the unusually wide High Street of the town of Moreton-in-Marsh has always been busy with traffic between the Midlands and the south-west. These days the traffic is more intense and rows of stone-built shops, houses and coaching inns face each other across the busy highway. Moreton grew as a market town in the 1220s, and 18th century turnpike road building increased the town's prosperity. Many of the fine buildings in the High Street date from this period.

Once surrounded by low-level, swampy land, the town was flooded on occasions which may explain the present name (never **the** Marsh!). In 1868 the Fosse Way was raised and the fields drained.

Mann Institute

Curfew Tower

White Hart Royal Hotel

High Street

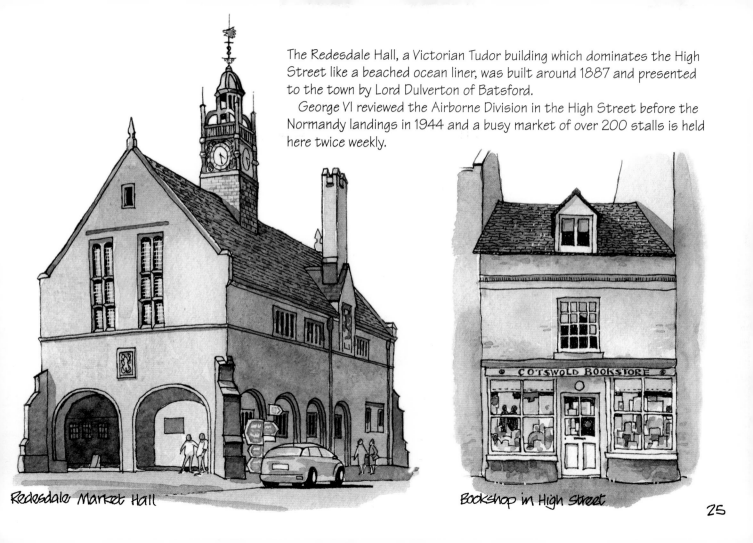

The Redesdale Hall, a Victorian Tudor building which dominates the High Street like a beached ocean liner, was built around 1887 and presented to the town by Lord Dulverton of Batsford.

George VI reviewed the Airborne Division in the High Street before the Normandy landings in 1944 and a busy market of over 200 stalls is held here twice weekly.

Redesdale Market Hall

Bookshop in High Street

25

The Steps

Curfew Tower

The Steps, a striking Palladian townhouse at the southern end of High Street, was built in the mid-18th century. The Curfew Tower, on the corner of Oxford Street, dates back to the Norman Conquest. The bell, dated 1633, was rung nightly until the 1860s to order people back to their homes to 'cover fire' for the night. It was also at one time the town's 'lock-up' (jail).

There's a car park along the centre of the High Street with a number of attractive and interesting buildings to enjoy, and a series of well-stocked antiques shops to browse.

Houses in High street

NOTGROVE   *3 miles north of Northleach*

A small, upland village of well-restored cottages, Notgrove is spread thinly around a sloping green and belongs to one private estate. The Norman church and rebuilt manor house lie up the hill on the southern edge at the end of a long driveway of pollarded trees. There's a car park at the village hall.

The Stone Age burial chambers of Notgrove Long Barrow are a mile away. Earth covering the lonely site was removed in a 1934 excavation, exposing some massive stonework.

cottage overlooking the green

Cotswold 'longhouse' on the green

UPPER SLAUGHTER *2 miles south-west of Stow-on-the-Wold*

Warm Cotswold stone cottages, re-modelled by Lutyens in 1906 and grouped around a small square look picturesque enough, but the lane that rises past Upper Slaughter church unexpectedly dips into a scene of blissful Englishness. A ford crosses the gentle River Eye (known locally as Slaughter Brook) beneath a single, magnificent, sycamore tree. To the left, across an acre of mown grass, stands the Manor House, one of the finest examples of Elizabethan architecture in the Cotswolds. Little stone bridges cross the brook, fringed by wildflowers and rushes.
This is a special place.

The Square & St Peter's Church

UPPER SLAUGHTER
Ford
Church
PARKING in square
River Eye
Footpath
Mill
LOWER SLAUGHTER
Church
Road to Upper Slaughter
Ford
To Bourton-on-the-Water

Upper Slaughter is conveniently laid out for an circular walk and the mile-long stroll along the banks of the river to the neighbouring village of Lower Slaughter is highly recommended.

The ford on the River Eye

Typical stone slab bridge

St Peter's church

St Peter's church, originally Norman, has suffered many restorations, but contains a brass to John Slaughter (1583) whose family built the Manor House in the 16th century. Far from its brutal connotation, 'Slaughter' is possibly derived from an Old English word meaning 'slough' or 'boggy place'.

Apart from somewhere to park (and the scenery), the village has no amenities for casual visitors.

Upper Slaughter is one of the few double 'thankful villages' in England and Wales – all the men it sent to fight in the first and second World Wars returned home safely. Upper Slaughter has much to be thankful for.

29

LOWER SLAUGHTER

1 mile south-east of Upper Slaughter

Lower Slaughter is the epitome of Cotswold charm, with stone houses winding along the banks of leisurely River Eye, crossed by a series of delightful small stone bridges and overhung at the east end by graceful willows. But thankfully for the discerning visitor, the small, trim village has wisely not been allowed to over-commercialise its many attractions. Even the excellent village shop is discretely tucked away beside the bakehouse at the rear of the old mill. The 19th century corn mill has a working waterwheel and is now a museum. Its red-brick chimney stands out in striking contrast to the mellow, honey-coloured walls of the late 16th and early 17th century houses.

Doorway overlooking
Slaughter Brook

The Mill

The owner of the quarry at Little Barrington, Valentine Strong, built Lower Slaughter Manor House during the 1650's. The Manor is now a luxury hotel and a popular venue for society and show-biz weddings. St Mary's church was built next door in 1867, with an impressive spire.

Lower Slaughter has been accused of being no more than a 'Cotswold set-piece' but the efforts to keep it 'unspoilt' are admirable. Even the modern council houses have traditional Cotswold stone roofs. Parking in the village is difficult.

The bridge over Slaughter Brook -
the photographer's favourite view

31

SNOWSHILL   *2 miles south of Broadway*

Overlooking the Avon valley and the Midland Plain, Snowshill is a wonderfully disordered village, built on a hillside so that hardly a building is on the same level as its neighbour.

Its history stretches back over 1,000 years. The King of Mercia gave the manor to the Abbey of Winchcombe, where it remained until the Dissolution, when it was given to Katherine Parr, the sixth wife of King Henry VIII.

St Barnabas church, at the centre of the village, was solidly rebuilt in 1864 with enormously thick walls.

With an array of ancient and unspoilt traditional Cotswold cottages and its open aspect, Snowshill is a delight to explore. The peaceful valleys and windswept hills of the surrounding countryside are equally good for walkers or riding enthusiasts.

17c cross

St Barnabas' church

The Snowshill Arms dates from the 13th century and is a traditional village inn which welcomes all-comers, particularly, according to its website, 'our American cousins'. The village has no other facilities.

Snowshill Arms

looking east across the village

Snowshill Manor

Snowshill Manor, built in traditional Cotswold style with a William & Mary front during the 1500s, is packed with bygone curios; toys, tools, musical instruments, even bicycles. They are the lifetime collection of an eccentric magpie, Charles Paget Wade, who lived in a cottage in the grounds, refused every modern amenity and slept in a Tudor cupboard-bed. He donated the Manor to the National Trust in 1951 and it's now open to the public.

STANTON *2.5 miles south-west of Broadway*

An outstandingly beautiful estate village snuggled below wooded
Shenberrow Hill, Stanton was lovingly restored by Sir Philip Stott, who
owned the manor from 1906 to 1937. Local stone houses line the long main
street in homogeneous perfection as it climbs to the hospitable Mount Inn,
from where there's a terrific view back across the village rooftops.

St Michael's church is tucked away up an alley behind the medieval village
cross. Of Norman origins, the interior of the building was severely damaged
during the Civil War when, like other Cotswold churches, it was used to
house prisoners.

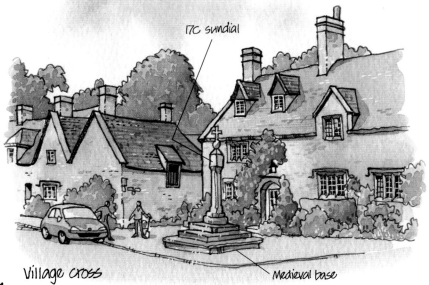

17C sundial

Village cross

Medieval base

Sheppey Corner

A magnificent converted barn stands near the road junction at the centre of the village which is still known as Sheppey Corner from the time when sheep from the hills were gathered here for shearing. There are some good walks with fantastic views over Shenberrow Hill to Snowshill or along the Cotswold Way to the neighbouring estate village of Stanway.

Barn conversion

St Michael's church

Stanton is a quiet village with no tourist attractions other than the beauty of its weathered stone buildings and cared-for gardens. But who could wish for more?

STANWAY *4 miles south-west of Broadway*

Stanway House gatehouse

A huge Jacobean manor house, Stanway House, dominates the area. It was built around 1600 by Sir Paul Tracy after abbey land was acquired at the Dissolution. The same family have lived in the house ever since with only a short break.

The house is open to the public and has a magnificent tithe barn built around 1370, a remarkable 60-pane full height bay window and a restored water garden with the highest gravity-fed fountain in the world, which can reach a height of 300 feet when all the valves are open. An 'own brew' beer, Stanway, is brewed on the premises and sold in local pubs.

The gateway to the house is oddly built at the side of the house rather than at the front entrance. Its flamboyant design was for years attributed to Inigo Jones, but is now thought to be the work of a local mason, Timothy Strong.

Cricket pavilion

A thatched cricket pavilion, clad with larch poles and raised on saddle stones is a surprising sight in the parkland surroundings at the edge of the village. It was presented to Stanway by J.M. Barrie, the author of *Peter Pan*, who was a keen cricketer and a frequent visitor to Stanway House during the early 1900s. A local 'fairy' story has it that moonlight flickering on his bedroom wall inspired Barrie's creation of Tinkerbell.

Stanway is only a tiny estate village, hidden away beneath the woods of Stanway Hill, but it's rich in beauty, interest and jaw-dropping oddities.

Parking is possible at the church but, apart from Stanway House, the village has no facilities.

The classic, chocolate-box Cotswold scene

37

LOWER SWELL
0.5 miles west of Stow-on-the-Wold

Situated on the banks of the River Dikler just down the hill from Stow-on-the-Wold, the tidy little village of Lower Swell gathers around a triangular green on a minor road near the village hall. Most of the buildings, even the new ones, are of stone and many have Cotswold stone roofs. The oldest surviving houses are 17th century, including the Golden Ball Inn which sells locally brewed Donnington Ale.

There are usually places to park with consideration around the green. Apart from the pub, the village has no visitor facilities.

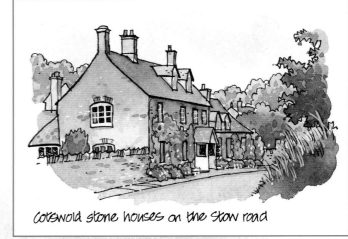

Cotswold stone houses on the Stow road

village hall

War memorial designed by Sir Edwin Lutyens

The Green

38

UPPER SWELL
0.5 miles north of Stow-on-the-Wold

The quiet, little village of Upper Swell is spread down a hill to the River Dikler where a three arched 18th century bridge still carries traffic on the B4077 road to Stow. An early 19th century mill with its waterwheel intact stands by the bridge, from where you can see a moss-covered weir and the large mill pond beyond. A row of attractive 18th century houses are attached to the mill.

Parking in the village is difficult – a lay-by beyond the bridge is a good bet – and there are no amenities.

Mill pond of the River Dikler

The Mill

18th century bridge

The main road through the village

A lane from the north end of Upper Swell takes you to a terrific view over the picturesque Donnington Brewery. The River Dikler rises on the private brewery estate, but has been damned to form a lake which drives a large mill wheel. The buildings housed a corn mill in the 13th century and were later used by cloth weavers.

Donnington Ales have been on sale throughout the Cotswolds since 1865 and the brewery now supplies its own 15 tied houses and a number of local free houses with quality 'real ale'.

39

WINCHCOMBE

7 miles south-west of Broadway

Sheltered on three sides by high Cotswolds hills, the market town of Winchcombe is situated along the western bank of the River Isbourne. With old cottages, small shops, a rich history and some good pubs and tea-rooms, there's plenty for the visitor to enjoy.

During Saxon times, the town was the important wool capital of Mercia, a separate shire. Later it became the site of one of the largest Benedictine monasteries in England and a place of pilgrimage for the rich and powerful.

During the Dissolution, the abbey was totally destroyed and not a trace of it remains above ground. With the resultant loss of pilgrims and employment, Winchcombe was plunged into poverty. The townsfolk turned to crafts to make a living, even growing tobacco for a while.

Somehow the town survived and is now a largely unspoilt and bustling place where butchers, bakers and greengrocers shops can all still be found.

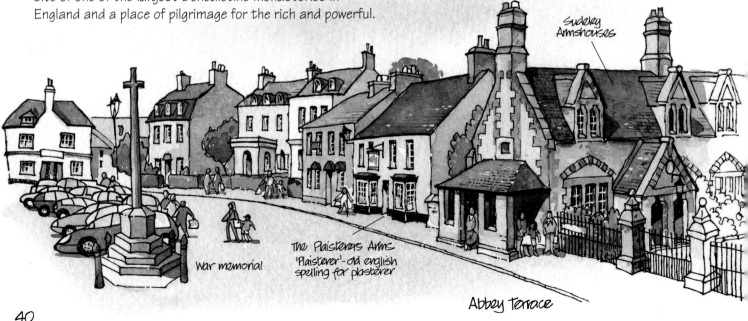

Sudeley Almshouses

War memorial

The Plaisterers Arms
'Plaisterer'- old english spelling for plasterer

Abbey Terrace

17C White Lion in North Street

The Town Hall in the High Street was brick-built in Tudor style in 1853 and enlarged in 1871. The High Street narrows into Hailes Street which has several more Tudor houses with exposed timber-framing and overhung first floors.

North Street has some interesting buildings, including the 17th century White Lion and an old brewery house. During the reign of King Richard II a horse market was held along this street, where iron rings for the tethering of horses can still be seen. Gloucester Street, at the west end of the town beyond the church, is also tightly-packed with ancient buildings.

The cheery Sudeley Almshouses, built in 1865 off Abbey Terrace to a design by Sir Gilbert Scott, are a delight with their patterns of different coloured stone.

There's also a wonderful string of cottages on Vineyard Street (the abbey once had a vineyard — those monks knew how to live!) going down to the river where a ducking stool for 'gossipers' was kept at the waterside during the 18th century.

The Town Hall in High Street

Jacobean House & St Peter's Church

Jacobean House, in a small square near the church, is a superb example of a typical 17th century merchant's house.

Great House, a 17th century house with a hipped Cotswold stone roof, is a striking sight down the hill off the High Street.

Winchcombe is an excellent base for walkers, with the Cotswold Way, Gloucester Way and Wychavon Way all passing through the town. There are also some fine hiking routes around the surrounding hills.

In an early example of a private and public joint building project, the chancel of the large Perpendicular church of St Peter was built by the abbey around the 1460s, and the parish was responsible for building the nave. Despite the involvement of the abbey, the church miraculously survived the Dissolution. An altar cloth, said to have been stitched by Catherine of Aragon, first wife of Henry VIII, when she visited Sudeley Castle, is displayed in the church. There are 40 gargoyles around the building's exterior, probably representing local town characters from the 1460s.

Great House in Castle Street

The galleried yard of the George Inn

Across the river from Winchcombe, Sudeley Castle is renowned for 1,000 years of royal history and its beautiful gardens.

Anne Boleyn, the second of Henry VIII's wives, visited Sudeley and Catherine Parr, his sixth and last wife came to live here after his death in 1547. She quickly remarried but died in childbirth in 1549.

The Dent family acquired the almost derelict castle in 1837 and Emma Dent is responsible for much of its restoration. She also provided the town with its first piped water supply to celebrate Queen Victoria's Golden Jubilee.

Sudeley castle gatehouse

The George Hotel, across the road from the town hall in the High Street, is the most interesting of the pre-reformation domestic buildings surviving in the town. It was built by the abbey as an inn for its pilgrims. The doorway has carved in its spandrels the initials of Abbot Richard Kidderminster, who resigned due to ill health in 1525. An open gallery has been preserved in the narrow courtyard behind.

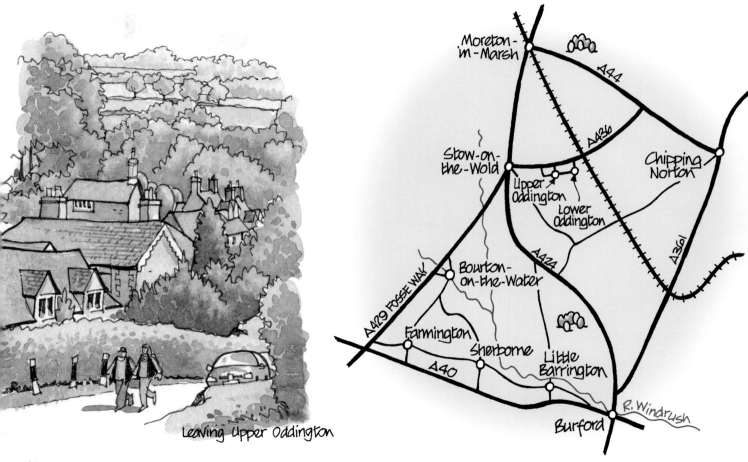

Leaving Upper Oddington

THE NORTH-EAST

As you move eastwards, the landscape becomes less wooded and more exposed, still hilly but with more individual hills rather than the single long escarpment that runs along the western side.

Stow-on-the-Wold, the main cross-roads in the area, sits appropriately on the top of the largest hill. Farmland rises and falls through the Oddingtons, oddly well-named and off the beaten track, but still worth visiting, if only to peer through your fingers at the Doom paintings in the 12th century church at Lower Oddington.

Chipping Norton is in Oxfordshire, but the bustling market town with the most amazing mill building in the Cotswolds is far too good to exclude. Burford is also in Oxfordshire, the widely accepted 'Southern gateway to the Cotswolds' that no visitor should miss.

The River Windrush flows attractively through Burford and upstream through Little Barrington and the parkland at Sherborne. The lane from Burford to Farmington is a delight to travel, with hills on one side and the Windrush winding its way though the trees on the other. Farmington is a surprising little place with a magnificent sycamore on the green shading a tiny pumphouse.

Finally, in this section, there's Bourton-on-the-Water, the region's premier tourist village which, like Burford, every Cotswold lover should visit. Maybe not for the same reasons – or possibly more than once.

lane near Sherborne

BOURTON-ON-THE-WATER

3 miles south of Stow-on-the-Wold

The most commercialised of all the Cotswold villages, Bourton-on-the-Water still manages to wear its mantle of 'set-piece visitor mecca' with some style and grace. It's unashamedly 'pretty', with a series of ornamental bridges spanning the shallow waters of the River Windrush along a tree-shaded green.

High street gift shops

Motor Museum

Bourton has a number of attractive buildings, many adapted for the business of tourism but mostly avoiding the adoption of garish shop fronts and signs. It also has a number of well-established visitor attractions, discretely hidden away, but all well worth a visit.

The Motor Museum is housed in an old watermill at the northern end of the green. Though its main focus is on motoring, the museum is full of the everyday paraphernalia that made motoring such a pleasure, including picnic sets from the 1920s, caravans, radio sets – and knitted swimsuits!

Bourton's fascinating Model Village is sited in the garden of the Old New Inn and is a perfect one-ninth miniature in stone of Bourton itself. It was built by an earlier inn-owner with a small team of local craftsmen during the early 1930s and opened on the Coronation day of King George VI and Queen Elizabeth in 1937. The Model Village includes a model of itself with its own miniature Windrush, around ten centimetres wide, running through it.

Mill Bridge

High Bridge

Bourton's bridges and the canal-like look of the Windrush have led to the village being tagged, somewhat fancifully, 'Venice of the Cotswolds'. However, the bridges are delightful and some are surprisingly old.

Mill Bridge, a road bridge at the western end of the village, was built in 1654, replacing a ford and originally called Broad or Big Bridge.

High Bridge, a footbridge at the centre of the green, dates back to 1756.

47

Payne Bridge

New Bridge

Coronation Bridge

Payne Bridge is another foot-crossing, dated 1776.

New Bridge was built in 1911 by a local benefactor, George Frederick Moore, a successful tea-planter who did much to enhance the appearance of the green.

Coronation Bridge, opposite the Old New Inn, was built in 1953, replacing an earlier wooden structure dating back to 1750.

The Windrush is one of the Bourton's most cherished features. Fish dart through the clear water and a gaggle of ducks is always on hand to delight the children.

St Lawrence's church

St Lawrence's church is one of the few examples in the Cotswolds of a Norman church built on completely demolished Saxon foundations. The present building has a 14th century chancel, a Georgian tower and Victorian nave. A lead-covered dome on the tower has a vaguely Eastern influenced. The juxtaposition of styles may be interesting and historic, but pretty it isn't.

There's a large visitor car park at the southern end of the village on Rissington Road, close to Birdland Park and Gardens. Located in a former trout farm on the Windrush, Birdland is home for over 500 birds, including penguins, pelicans and pheasants.

Bourton-on-the-Water can be unpleasantly over-crowded and may not always be everyone's favourite day out in the Cotswolds, but on a bright day, out of season, the village has a lot going for it.

Gift shop in a traditional building

A rest beside the Windrush

49

BURFORD

9 miles south-east of Stow-on-the-Wold

Considered by many to be the southern entrance to the Cotswolds, Burford's broad High Street slopes gracefully down from the wolds to the willow-fringed River Windrush and an inviting view of open countryside beyond.

No two buildings in the High Street are the same. It's a kaleidoscope of old grey-gabled houses, shops, tearooms, hotels and inns, some with wonderfully crooked walls, and a roof line of higgledy-piggledy delight.

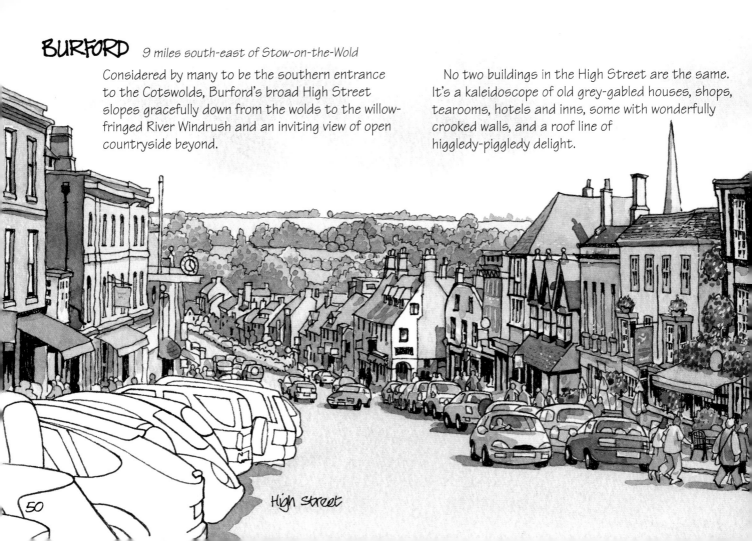

High Street

Medieval bridge over the Windrush

The 15th century bridge at the bottom of the High Street has so far resisted the pressures of highway improvers, and motorists still have to queue at traffic lights to cross.

Burford was built on the wealth from wool, quarrying and coaches. In the 18th century it was an important stop on the Oxford to London route, when as many as forty coaches passed through in a day. 'Beware the Burford Bait' was a warning not to overeat in the many inns. With the number of tempting teashops in today's town the lure of 'Burford Bait' is still thriving.

Tolsey Museum

15c refurbished coaching inn

Cob Hall

Tolls were once paid at the Tolsey, a 16th century room built on stone pillars. Its clock is held out to the street as if time was important in this timeless setting. The building is now a small museum and until the early 20th century the town fire engine was kept below it.

The oldest part of Burford lies between the bridge and Sheep Street. Cob Hall, so called because it was once the Swan Inn (a cob is an adult male swan), was first recorded in 1590.

Burford is built of oolite limestone from quarries on the eastern edge of the Cotswolds, the same stone of some of England's finest buildings, including Blenheim Palace and St Paul's Cathedral.

15c spire

Norman tower

Church of St John the Baptist

Houses in Sheep Street

St John the Baptist's church dates back to the 12th century with its tower heightened and the tall spire added towards the end of the 14th century. The magnificent south porch has an elegant tracery-panelled facade.

The nearby almshouses on Church Green, just outside the churchyard, were founded by Warwick the King-Maker when he was Lord of the Manor of Burford, and rebuilt in 1826. Nearby Church Lane has a public car park where you can join a tranquil footpath along the riverside.

Turn off the High Street at the Tolsey to see some lovely houses in Sheep Street and an old brewery building, now housing a tourist information bureau. The famous magazine 'The Countryman' was for many years edited from premises in this street.

AROUND BURFORD

Hops & Vines - glassware & home brewing

Town crest on an ancient building

Doorway of Church Green almshouses

Doorways in High Street

CHIPPING NORTON

8 miles south-east of Moreton-in-Marsh

The highest town in Oxfordshire and the most eastern outpost of the Cotswolds, Chipping Norton is situated on the western slopes of a hillside overlooking the Common Brook, a tributary of the River Evenlode.

'Chippy', as the bustling town in known locally, has never let tourism get in the way of everyday life and has 'proper' shops and a amiable air of normality not found in some of the Cotswold set pieces.

There's been a market here since the 13th century and during the 15th century the town was a major wool-trading centre. A terrace of impressive 17th-19th century hotels, inns and shops head the square, which is now mainly given over to parking, but a market is still held every Wednesday.

The Town Hall in Market Place

The Blue Boar

Traditional butcher's shop

North side of the Town Hall

Built in 1842, the Palladian style Town Hall dominates the Market Place and is a proud symbol of the days when the town was a borough. Apart from council business, which ended in 1857, the building has seen service as a lock-up, market, corn exchange and entertainment hall. It also once housed a weighbridge for coal and was the garage for the town fire engine. It's now used for corporate events and marriages.

56

The Bliss Tweed Mill, Chipping Norton's most striking landmark, has been said to resemble a cross between a country mansion and a folly. It was built in 1872 and designed by George Woodhouse, a Lancashire architect. The building's dominant feature is a 165 feet-high chimney stack rising from a ribbed leaded dome, which looks remarkably like a giant sink plunger.

The mill closed in the early 1980s but reopened a few years later, converted to 34 luxury apartments on five floors.

William Bliss was instrumental in bringing the railway to Chipping Norton to supply coal for his mill's steam engines. The railway closed in the 1960s.

Bliss Tweed Mill

57

FARMINGTON

1.5 miles north-east of Northleach

A small village on high ground between the Leath and Sherborne valleys, Farmington is remarkably peaceful, considering how close it is to the A40 and the Fosse Way.

The handsome church of St Peter is largely Norman, restored with stone from the local quarry, situated high on the wolds above the village. The tower was added in the 15th century.

Pumphouse on the green

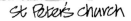

St Peter's church

A magnificent sycamore on Farmington Green shades a little octagonal pumphouse, built with eight gables and a small cupola in 1874. In 1935, the citizens of Farmington, Connecticut, USA, paid for a new stone roof to commemorate the 300th anniversary of the State of Connecticut.

You can park around the green but the village has no facilities for visitors.

Typical Cotswold idyll

LITTLE BARRINGTON *3 miles west of Burford*

A collection of stone cottages in the Windrush valley, gathered around a sloping green with a languid stream running through it, Little Barrington is a scene of Cotswold perfection.

Though all in harmony, each house is subtly different from the other, some with renovated medieval stone doorways. The large green was once a stone quarry and The Inn for All Seasons up the road on the A40 was originally built for the numerous quarrymen who worked in the area.

You can park at the green and a walk around it is highly recommended. There's another inn, The Fox, a half mile away, overlooking an old bridge over the Windrush. Apart from its fine hostelries, the village has no facilities.

the village

LOWER ODDINGTON
2.5 miles east of Stow-on-the-Wold

Situated just off the A436 road, where high ground around Stow dips to the River Evenlode, Lower Oddington lies off the beaten track and is untouched by tourism. Refurbished stone cottages with pretty gardens line the long main street and the former post office carries a plaque, HRK 1728.

There are two fine houses at the east end of the village. Oddington House, built around 1600 and enlarged around 1810, was formerly the family seat of the Chamderlaynes. The nearby Old Rectory dates back to the early 17th century.

Bellcotes on Holy Ascension church

East end of the village

Main Street

church of St Nicholas

Lower Oddington's most remarkable feature is the isolated but much loved 12th century church of St Nicholas, situated in a woodland setting half a mile down the track to Bledington Heath.

Inside the church, enormous 14th century Day of Judgement paintings cover an entire wall. This is real fire and brimstone religious imagery, common in many ancient churches but usually removed by prudish Victorian restoration. These paintings probably escaped as St Nicholas's was abandoned when a new parish church was built in the village. They were covered with whitewash during the Reformation which was removed by the vicar, Thomas Hodson, in 1912.

In total contrast to the church, the 16th century Fox Inn, clad in Virginia Creeper, provides all the modern comforts you would expect from a Cotswold pub. The village has no other facilities.

The Fox Inn

61

UPPER ODDINGTON

2 miles east of Stow-on-the-Wold

Unlike its linear, strung-out neighbour, Upper Oddington is a small, compact village set in a fold in the hills. The Cotswold stone houses and their mature, cared-for gardens make an attractive picture gathered around a circle of narrow lanes, garnished generously with trees.

The Horse & Groom dates back to 1580. Then a simple hostelry, it's now a classy 'gastro-pub' using locally sourced produce.

There are several large and desirable properties in a cul-de-sac near a small green on the lane to Lower Oddington. Apart from the Horse and Groom, the village has no facilities.

Road into the village

Horse & Groom village inn

62

SHERBORNE 4 miles south of Bourton-on-the-Water

Built of grey-stone along Sherborne Brook, a tributary of the Windrush, Sherborne is part of the Sherborne House Estate on the valley road between Burford and Northleach.

Winchcombe Abbey owned the estate during the middle ages. The Dutton family acquired it in 1551 and by 1651 they had built Sherborne House. The family bequeathed the estate to the National Trust in the 1980s and the house has been divided into luxury flats. The land is now a large park, open to the public with walks, old farm buildings and a sculpture trail. There are also a picnic area and a small shop. The village has no other facilities.

In Lodge Park, a couple of miles away and also open to the public, there's a rare 17th century grandstand, built by John Dutton. Looking more like a beautiful little house than a modern grandstand, the Lodge originally had rooms to stay in but was primarily erected to watch the contemporary pastime of the rich, the coursing of deer by greyhounds.

Private courtyard for luxury flats

Sherborne House

Former post office

Terrace of cottages

63

STOW-ON-THE-WOLD
4 miles south of Moreton-in-Marsh

At 790ft (240m) above sea level, Stow is the highest town in the Cotswolds and if legend is to be believed, the windiest. It's well placed at the junction of eight roads, one of them the Roman Fosse Way. The remarkably large Market Square bears testament to the town's heritage as a major sheep market. Daniel Defoe recorded that 20,000 sheep were once sold here in a single day. Henry II granted the town a market charter in 1107 and changed the name from Edwardstow.

Market Square

Modern Stow is still centred on the square, with a variety of inns, eating houses, retail outlets, inns and a treasure trove of eclectic antique shops. Though attracting many visitors, it remains refreshingly 'untouristy'.

St Edward's Hall was built in 1878, paid for partly by funds left unclaimed in the town's Savings Bank. The belfry tower was added in 1894 to house the fire bell as the rector of the church wouldn't allow the church bell to be used. It's now the public library and a small museum.

Use of the stocks, in which criminals were once locked and exposed to public ridicule or assault, dates back to the 15th century, though it's doubtful if those displayed at Stow have ever been used in anger.

Markets are still held regularly in the square. During the summer months it's a good place to enjoy one of the most endearing and baffling symbols of eccentric 'Englishness' – Morris dancers!

The stocks

St Edward's Hall

St Edward's church

ST EDWARDS   CAFE

St Edward's House

St Edward's House, at the top of the square, looks ancient with its worn stonework and twin fluted Corinthian pilasters, but was actually built in the early 18th century.

THE KINGS ARMS   HOTEL POSTING-HOUSE

The Kings Arms

Sit on the base of the medieval cross in the Market Place and you are sitting where Sir Jacob Astley did when he surrendered his Royalist Army to end the English Civil War. The nearby King's Arms, was a flourishing coaching inn as early as 1647, with a reputation as the best between London and Worcester. King Charles I famously stayed here before the Battle of Naseby in 1645 and it was the location for the BBC's TV adaption of the Thomas Hardy novel, *The Mayor of Casterbridge*.

The Royalist Hotel

The Royalist Hotel at the bottom of Digbeth Street has been certified as the oldest inn in England, dating from 947AD and authenticated in the *Guinness Book of Records*. There's a 'witch-mark' in a fireplace to ward off evil spirits and a frieze in a bedroom which dates from the Crusades.

In 1646, the town became the site of the last battle in the first of the English Civil Wars. A royalist army, marching through the region in a desperate attempt to join the king at Oxford, was halted by parliamentary forces at Stow. The battle was bloody and ended with 1,000 royalists being imprisoned in St Edward's church.

In 1657, the church was declared ruinous but by the end of the 1800s was largely restored and is now a haven of peace off the busy square. The 88ft-high tower boasts the heaviest peel of bells in all of Gloucestershire. In the south aisle there's a large painting of the Crucifixion by Gaspar de Craeyer (1582-1669).

Lanes off the square were made narrow and winding to control the sheep and are, with the rest of this engaging town, well worth exploring.

St Edward's church

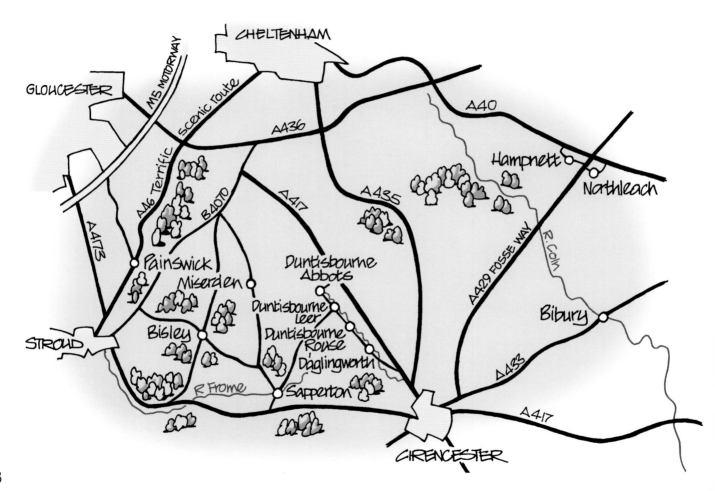

CHELTENHAM

GLOUCESTER

M5 MOTORWAY

A46 Terrific Scenic route

A436

A40

Hampnett

Northleach

A4173

B4070

A417

A435

A429 FOSSE WAY

R. Colm

Painswick

Miserden

Duntisbourne Abbots

Duntisbourne Leer

Duntisbourne Rouse

Bibury

Bisley

Daglingworth

STROUD

R Frome

Sapperton

A433

A417

CIRENCESTER

68

THE SOUTH

Like most north and south comparisons, the Cotswolds are softer and more sophisticated in the south.

Hampnett, scattered and peaceful, and Northleach, a compact and bustling market town, are set on an open hillside along the A40. Bibury, part of the tourist coach circuit, could be the Bourton-on-the-Water of the south but set in a wooded valley along the River Coln, the village is far too genteel for that.

Moving west of Cirencester across the A417 road, the three small Duntisbourne settlements strung along a relaxed brook are picturesque places where nothing much happens except the slow passage of time. Daglingworth, at the southern end of the brook, is slightly busier but still not a place where anyone rushes. Further west to Sapperton, we're into the broad wooded valley of the River Frome, so dramatic in autumn colours it's know as the Golden Valley.

Bisley, on high ground north of the valley, is a delight to explore and Miserden even further north is a splendid example of a well-preserved estate village. Finally there's Painswick, the finest town in this area, where the stone is silver grey and the architecture elegant. The A46 road to Painswick from Brockworth is one of the finest scenic roads in the Cotswolds with fantastic views to the horseshoe bend in the River Severn, and a great place to picnic on Painswick Hill.

The Painswick stream valley near Paradise

BIBURY

6 miles north-east of Cirencester

Set in a shallow but steep-sided valley of River Coln, the agreeable small village of Bibury tries to live up to William Morris' excessive description as 'surely the most beautiful in Britain' with some success.

Arlington Row, a row of nine Cotswold weavers' cottages, are so admired that Henry Ford wanted to export them to America. Thankfully, they were saved for restoration in 1930. The weavers supplied cloth for fulling at Arlington Mill across the water meadow. The earliest of the cottages dates to around 1380 and they are now owned by the National Trust.

water meadow

70   Arlington Row

17C footbridge over the Coln

The Coln runs shallow through the village and is so full of fish and water weed there's barely room for all the ducks and moorhens. It's crossed by attractive footbridges and a 1770 road bridge.

The ivy-clad Swan Hotel dates to around 1800. There is also a large trout farm and gardens alongside the river, which may explain the abundance of fish in the Coln.

Arlington Mill was rebuilt on its Domesday site in the late 18th century as a cloth and corn mill. Stone buttresses were added in 1859 when steam engines were installed. It's now a museum and gallery.

St Mary's church has Saxon features and is surrounded by fine houses. The village is on the coach tour circuit and becomes extremely busy, with parking difficult.

Bibury has a lot of charm and William Morris wasn't all wrong. But he wasn't all right either.

Swan Hotel & 18c road bridge

Arlington Mill

High Street

BISLEY   *3.5 miles east of Stroud*

A large but compact village sitting at the head of a combe high on the wolds overlooking the Golden Valley of the River Frome, Bisley has a wonderful setting and a striking mix of fine Cotswold architecture, from cottages to large houses.

Bisley is a typical example of the steep hill villages near Stroud. Row upon row of stone houses rise each side of the long and narrow High Street like an impressive ampitheatre. The street is too narrow for tourist coaches and it's difficult to park a car without getting in someone's way. There are no front gardens and the houses are flush with the pavement.

The village grew with the Cotswold wool trade and later there was work in the textile mills along the Frome, but during the mid-19th century the area suffered great poverty. Bisley survived and is now largely a peaceful commuter village for Stroud.

Wells Road

BISLEY BRITISH LEGION

There's much to enjoy in the long High Street and some wonderful surprises. Look out for the old Bell Inn, built around 1687 and restored for the British Legion in 1953, with impressive carved stonework over the doorway.

Norwich House

Bisley Wells

From the lychgate of the church, restored in 1896, there's a fabulous view to the other side of the narrow valley where a terrace of stone cottages climb over the steep hillside.

Sinegar Square, on the High Street below the church, has the tree-shaded former police station and next door, Wesley House, the 19th century home of Sister Amelia and other Wesleyan sisters who ran a mission to provide holidays for deprived children from London.

The famous Bisley Wells are down a lane below the steep churchyard. Five springs issue from an elegant stone semicircle while two others flow into stone cattle troughs. They were restored by Thomas Keble, brother of the rector, in 1863. Each year local children dress the wells with flowers in his memory.

All Saint's church has an imposing spire and a unique Poor Soul's Light in the churchyard. The 13th century stone structure is thought to have been used to hold candles for masses to be said for the redemption of the souls of the poor. It's believed to be the only outdoor example of its kind in England.

Sinegar Square

The Bear Inn at the top of George Street has 17th century columns supporting the upper floor. At one time it was owned by one of Nelson's captains and has a 58ft deep well in the cellar and a mysterious tunnel going towards the church. The inn was probably the old court house, as the village lock-up is nearby. Restored in 1998, it has two cells open to the elements – and no facilities.

Bear Inn & lock-up in George Street

All Saint's church lychgate

Apart from the Bear, the village has another public house, The Stirrup Cup, at the top of the High Street and there are a few small shops. Bisley is an unassuming place, full of interest, that can only be fully enjoyed on foot.

There are some fine walks from the village, particularly along the upper Toadsmoor Valley to Lypiatt Park or around the smaller valleys near Oakridge and France Lynch.

DUNTISBOURNE ABBOTS 5 miles north-west of Cirencester

The most northerly of the trio of small Duntisbourne villages strung along the Duntisbourne Brook, delightfully linked by narrow and winding lanes following the contours of the hills.

Duntisbourne Abbots has ancient origins but is now modernly trim, an idyllic spot, framed in a bowl of wooded hills with a lazy river and a saddleback-towered church on the hilltop. The brook was widened across the road so cart wheels could be cleaned and the ford now performs a similar function for horses hooves.

The village name comes from the original owners, the abbots of Gloucester. St Peter's church dates from the 12th century and has a picturesque lychgate.

St Peter's church

village centre

76

DUNTISBOURNE LEER
0.5 miles south-east of Duntisbourne Abbots

A hamlet notable for the 17th century farm buildings gathered so perfectly around a ford you'd think a modern ad agency had planned it and provided the ducks. There's a remarkable number of pigeon holes in one of the barns and the cottage across the water. The unusual name is derived from the Abbey of Lire in Normandy, to whom the manor belonged until 1416, when it was given to Cirencester Abbey.

Cottage with pigeon holes

Ford over the Duntisbourne Brook

Main road

DUNTISBOURNE ROUSE

One mile south-east of Duntisbourne Leer

St Michael's church

The third of the Duntisbourne settlements takes its name from the le Rouse family who were once Lords of the Manor. The quiet village is pleasant enough but is most interesting for its ancient church; small, simple and perfectly proportioned. Built on a hillside, there's an unusual crypt chapel beneath the Norman chancel. The 16th century tower has a saddleback roof.

The Duntisbourne area is prime walking country but there are no facilities.

DAGLINGWORTH

0.75 miles south-east of Duntisbourne Rouse

The ownership of this pleasant and peaceful village has changed repeatedly since Saxon times. Lately it's been part of the Duchy of Cornwall. The Saxon church, on a hill, has rare stone figures dated 1050. There's a small car park opposite the church, but no other facilities.

Main road

12c Daglingworth House

Church of the Holy Rood

SAPPERTON *5 miles west of Cirencester*

Set along a terrace high above the wooded Frome Valley, Sapperton enjoys spectacular views, especially when the woods are ablaze with autumn colours. The village was part of the late 19th century Arts and Crafts Movement and its leading lights designed many of the buildings at the east end of the village. St Kenelm's church snuggles into the hillside and has some Norman touches but was largely rebuilt during the 14th century. Some Jacobean woodwork was saved from Sapperton House when it was demolished around 1730. Apart from the hospitable Bell Inn, the village has no facilities.

The Coates portal of Sapperton tunnel

The Bell

St Kenelm's church

Sapperton Canal tunnel was opened in 1789 on the Thames and Severn Canal after five years of construction, mostly through solid rock. It's over two miles long and has no tow path. Narrowboats were propelled through it by 'legging': bargees laying on a plank across the boat and pushing with their legs on the walls or roof. The canal was superseded by the coming of the railway and fell into decay during the 1920s. It still isn't negotiable, but a trust runs tourist boat trips into the tunnel during the winter months. There's a public house at each end, The Tunnel House, near the Coates portal in the centre of Hailey Wood, and the Daneway Inn at the other.

HAMPNETT *1 mile north-west of Northleach*

Reached by a single track road off the A40, the Saxon settlement of Hampnett consists of an intriguing trio of sub-villages with a large field at their centre, near the source of the River Leach. The main village consists of a number of converted farm buildings gathered picturesquely around the church. St George's is mainly Norman and the muted colours of its exterior stone give no hint of the blaze of colour that awaits inside. The interior is decorated with amazing Victorian stencilling, painted in a floral design with angelic figures, the idea of the Rev Wiggins, vicar of Hampnett in 1868. The effect is startling and some of it, especially on the ribbed vaulting of the chancel, is quite beautiful.

The main village

A lane beyond the church goes down to an attractive row of Cotswold cottages and some large willow trees overhanging the infant River Leach. The through road rises to the top part of the village, which is no more than a sparse collection of houses with a rough green where you can park. The village has no facilities.

This is good walking country and a route along the lane to Turkdean is highly recommended. A steep bank of beautiful beech trees splits the small village into two parts, Upper and Lower Turkdean, and are a breath-taking sight in Autumn.

Barn conversion

Lane to the upper village

MISERDEN

6 miles north-east of Stroud

Tidy and unspoilt, Miserden is part of the 3,000 acre Miserden Estate. At the centre of the village, outside the Carpenter's Arms, a magnificent sycamore tree shades a circular seat from where you can admire the woods of Miserden Park, the seat of the Sandys family in Elizabethan times. The old house commands a spectacular position facing steep wooded valleys where the young waters of the River Frome meander among the trees.

The western approach

Village centre

Miserden is a thriving community with a church, pub, village hall, primary school and a post office. There's a local cricket club and various groups meet on a regular basis in the village hall.

In 1898, a group of Christian anarchists dedicated to living their lives according to the strictures of Leo Tolstoy bought land and built wooden houses a mile from Miserden. The Whiteway Colony still exists and a number of its early founders are buried in St Andrew's churchyard.

The drastically restored Saxon church contains some magnificent monuments including the effigies of Sir William Sandys and his wife carved in Derbyshire alabaster.

Miserden Park gardens are open to the public. A terrific walk from Bull Banks, south of the park, passes through glorious woods across to Duntisbourne Common and Edgeworth.

St Andrew's church

NORTHLEACH
8 miles south-west of Stow-on-the-Wold

One of the most important Cotswold wool towns, Northleach was founded during the 13th century at a commercially strategic point on the crossroads of the Fosse Way and the main road from Oxford to Gloucester, midway between Cirencester and Stow-on-the-Wold. For many years heavy traffic thundered through the narrow streets but the town is now bypassed by the A40.

High street

Walton House

During the Battle of Britain in 1940, RAF pilots of No. 87 Squadron were billeted in Walton House, a large old coaching inn in the High Street. They flew Hurricane fighter aircraft from a landing strip situated between Northleach and Bibury. At one time Walton House was a training stable and is said to be named after Walton, a descendant of a horse that won the Derby in 1787.

Butcher's shop in The Green

Northleach has suffered many ups and downs. It was hugely prosperous during the 15th century but suffered when the wool market declined. During the 18th century, coaching inns were established along the High Street to cater for the growing coach trade, of which The Red Lion and others are still public houses. With the growth of the railways, coaches disappeared. But as car ownership increased, the town again became a popular refreshment stop for travellers. It's now a pleasant and interesting place for visitors to enjoy traditional shops, historic buildings and Cotswold hospitality.

Overhung houses in West End

The Red Lion 85

Dubbed the 'Cathedral of the Cotswolds', the church of St Peter and St Paul, is so magnificent it's dedicated to two saints. The church was almost entirely rebuilt in the 15th century from the profits of the wool trade. It's a splendid example of the Perpendicular style with a huge tower and a much-admired, ornate south porch. Its treasures include a 15th century stone pulpit and a unique series of brasses of local wool merchants. The Cotswold wool men were powerful during the Middle Ages, not only in England but throughout Europe as a whole.

War memorial in Market Place

church of St Peter & St Paul

Clock on the Cotswold
Hall, West End

Houses in West End

The town's old buildings date mainly from the 16th and 17th centuries, with more exposed timber frames and overhung upper floors than is usual in this part Cotswolds.

The stark and still slightly scarey-looking, 'House of Correction' stands at the crossroads of the A40 and the Fosse Way on the edge of the town, designed in 1789 by the wonderfully named prison reformer, Sir George Onesiphorus Paul.

To best enjoy the town's attractions, park at the prison end of West End and walk its whole length into East End, with a detour for the Market Place, church and the Green. There's also a good country walk along the River Leach to Eastington.

Ancient wall on the
corner of Farmington Road

PAINSWICK *3 miles north of Stroud*

With its intricate pattern of narrow streets and elegant 17th and 18th century buildings of the local silver-grey stone and serenely set on a high spur above the Painswick Stream with views across a wooded valley to Bulls Cross, it's difficult to argue with Painswick's much-quoted title, 'Queen of the Cotswolds'.

From a cottage industry of spinning and weaving, the small town grew to an important cloth-making centre during the 16th century after Flemish weavers built fulling and finishing mills along the river. Huge prosperity funded the building of the town's finest buildings using stone quarried from nearby Painswick Beacon.

There's no obvious centre to Painswick. It's just a meandering maze of picturesque streets which are a delight for the visitor to explore.

BB

The only exposed timber framing in the town, though many of the houses are timbered inside

The post office

The Golden Heart Inn has long gone, but its beautiful wrought iron sign remains

GOLDEN HEART

Tibbiwell

St Mary's church is mostly 15th century with a radical restoration in the 19th century. The tall spire was added in 1632 and houses a peal of 12 bells, the oldest one donated in 1686.

The famous 'architecturally clipped' yew trees, scattered across the churchyard like a child's oversized sponge balls, were planted about 1792. Legend has it that if you try to count the trees you will always come to a different number. There are actually ninety-nine as, another legend has it, the devil always kills the hundredth.

The church was damaged by fire and vandalism during the Civil War and marks made by royalist cannonballs when parliamentary troops took refuge in the building are still visible below the clock face.

Painswick welcomes visitors. There's a handy car park in New Street, just below the churchyard.

Lightning can strike twice! The steeple was struck in 1763 and again in 1883.

The lychgate was built in 1901 using old timbers from the belfry. Appropriately, bells are carved on the bargeboards.

The beautiful church clockface, added in 2001

St Mary's church and lychgate

tea-caddy tomb

St Mary's churchyard contains a remarkable array of table tombs, the finest collection in the Cotswolds. Mostly 17th and 18th century, they were designed in the Renaissance tradition by expert stonemasons employed by wealthy clothiers. There's a huge variety of chest and pedestal tombs, known locally, for obvious reasons, as 'tea-caddies'. Cherubs, pie crust frills, scrolls and shells abound. The tombs are so well-loved, they have a local group dedicated to their preservation.

Our Lady & St Thérèse Roman Catholic church

Peaceful now after being converted from a slaughterhouse in 1934 and suffering World War !! bomb damage in 1941. The pretty cupola was added in 1954-56.

St Mary's Street beside the churchyard

PAINSWICK DOORWAYS

Town Hall, Victoria Square, dated 1840

Almshouse, dated 1924

Frederick Gyde was a great benefactor of the town, with a row of almshouses and an orphanage bearing his name. A street is also named in his honour.

Rossway House, New Street

Beacon House in New Street

The epitome of Painswick elegance and sophistication. The splendid Palladian style house was built for clothier Thomas Gardner in 1604. Dynevor House, next door, is dated 1801.

Tibbiwell Lane

which descends steeply to the converted fulling mills along Painswick Stream and some of the finest countryside in all of Gloucestershire.

The Cotswolds

The area lies on a band of oolite limestone arcing across England from Dorset to the Humber where the land has tilted up on its western side to form an escarpment with a gentle slope to the east. Designated 'An Area of Outstanding Natural Beauty' (AONB), the largest in England and Wales, the Cotswolds stretch 80 miles from Chipping Campden in the north, to Bath in the south, covering an area of 790 sq. miles and with 80 per cent of which is farmland. It has the largest number of conservation areas of any region and has been shaped by people for over 6000 years. The AONB has over 3,000 miles of public footpaths. Around 85,000 people live in the Cotswolds, one of the lowest population densities in England, with less than 300 residents in over half its parishes. The region attracts some 38 million day visitors a year, with tourism being the principle industry, generating over £130 million a year.

Cotswold stone

The Cotswolds are rich in oolitic limestone and so it was natural to start building with it in the Middle Ages due to its propensity and comparative cheapness. There are still quarries in the region extracting and working the stone for repairs and the construction of new buildings. The old limestone houses and cottages are invariably 'listed' buildings, which means they are strictly protected from alteration. The colour of the stone depends on where it was quarried. Generally, in the northern part of the Cotswolds the stone is honey golden brown and the further south it becomes more silvery in colour.

J.B. Priestley wrote of Cotswold stone: 'Even when the sun is obscured and the light is cold, these walls are still faintly warm and luminous, as if they knew the trick

The pumphouse at Farmington

of keeping the lost sunlight of centuries glimmering about them.'

The Cotswold Way

A long distance footpath between Chipping Campden in the north and Bath in the south. 102 miles long, It runs through prime Cotswold countryside along the escarpment and is well-marked and maintained. There are many other fine walks in the region

Fosse Way

A Roman road running through the Cotswolds, so called from the fosse or ditch that used to run along each side. It linked Exeter, in south-west England, with Lincoln in the East Midlands, and is now the A429.

Morris Dancing

Practiced in many parts of England but most commonly in the Cotswolds, Morris dancing is a folk dance performed outdoors – usually not far from a pub – by men wearing costumes consisting of white shirt and trousers, and a hat adorned with flowers and ribbon. Garters are worn around the legs with bells attached. Handkerchiefs or sticks are used in the dance and a fiddle or concertina provides the music. The dance often illustrates a legend or a rural activity such as sowing and harvesting, with the bells and handkerchiefs warding off evil spirits to ensure the fertility of the crops for the coming year.

Sheep

In the Middle Ages (5th to 15th centuries) the Cotswolds were well-known throughout Europe as the source of some of the best wool. The high wolds were ideal for

Village green at Upper Oddington

sheep and the abbeys and monasteries raised huge flocks of the 'Cotswold Lions'. These native sheep were large animals with long, golden fleeces. Wool merchants became enormously rich and spent much of their wealth on lavish church restoration as well as building fine houses for themselves. At that time 50 per cent of England's economy was based on wool.

Source of the River Thames
Most experts agree that the source of the Thames is in the Cotswolds but the precise location is a matter of hot debate. The traditional source is at Thames Head, north of Cirencester. It's a spring that only flows intermittently so there's also strong claims for Seven Springs, further north near Cheltenham, where the River Churn also rises. The alternative source would add another 14 miles to the river's 'official' 215-mile length.

Stone walls
The first great wall-building period in the Cotswolds was during the 18th century with the land enclosures. The second came in the 19th century when the land-owners build walls around their estates.
The walls are usually about two feet wide at the bottom and narrow to around fourteen inches at the top. The middle is filled with rubble and every so often a 'bonder' is put in as a strengthener and can be left sticking out to make a stile. At the required height, rows of stones are set upright to complete the wall. No cement or earth is used so air can permeate and the

construction remains dry. A properly built wall will last many hundreds of years with relatively little attention.

Thames & Severn Valley Canal
The canal was opened in 1789, linking the Stroudwater Canal at Stroud with the head of the navigable Thames at Lechgate, through the Sapperton Tunnel (see page 79). There were problems with leakage and an abnormal number of locks, but the canal's fate was sealed when the Great Western Railway was opened. The company bought the canal and stopped all traffic on it, allowing the waterway to become derelict. Its closure was one of the great tragedies of English canal history and although efforts are being made to reopen some sections, it's difficult to believe that this outstandingly beautiful link between the two great river systems will ever be reopened in its entirety.

Town or village?
When one becomes the other is a matter for debate. As a rough rule of thumb, towns have market squares and villages have greens.

Doorway at Blockley

Vernacular architecture
The Cotswolds building style is justifiably famous. It includes the use of local limestone in the walls and roof; a steeply pitched roof (60 degrees) usually with dormers; ridge tiles and coping; tall chimneys; large window sills of stone or wood; and detailed window mouldings of stone.

SOME ENGLISH HISTORY

The English Reformation
Part of a general discontent with the power of the Holy Roman Empire throughout Europe during the 16th century, the English reformation centred on Henry VIII's struggle with the Pope to have his marriage to Catherine of Aragon annulled so that he could marry his pregnant mistress, Anne Boleyn. The matter was resolved in 1533, when Thomas Cranmer, made Archbishop of Canterbury by the king, annulled the marriage and Catherine was forbidden to appeal to Rome. In 1534, on the King's instructions, parliament passed the Act of Supremacy, declaring him to be the Supreme Head of the English Church.

The Dissolution of the Monasteries (1536-40)
To complete the break with Rome, Henry VIII disbanded some 825 religious communities throughout England, Wales and Ireland. Abbeys, monasteries, priories, convents and friaries were destroyed and monastic land, around a third of all parishes, was seized by the Crown and quickly sold on, usually to the local gentry and nobility. The Dissolution is still the largest 'legal' transfer of property in English history since the Norman Conquest. It had a profound effect on the Cotswolds region which persists to this day.

The English Civil Wars (1642-49)
A series of armed conflicts between royalist supporters of King Charles I (Cavaliers) and the parliamentarians (Roundheads). The Cotswolds, a royalist-leaning region, became a battleground when the king set up headquarters at Oxford. The wars ended with the trial and execution of Charles I in 1649 and the establishment of a republic led by Oliver Cromwell.

Also in the Sketchbook series...

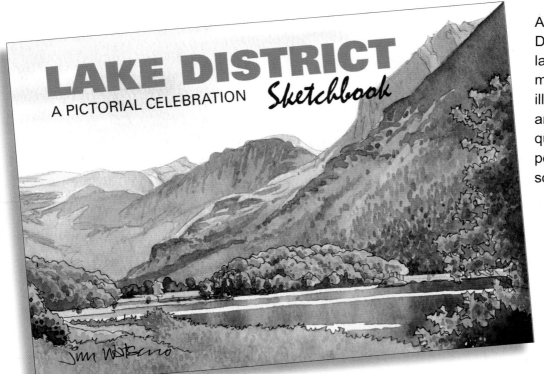

A tour of favourite Lake District towns, villages, lakes and dales with more than 200 colour illustrations, history, facts and figures, and a few quirky surprises. The perfect guidebook, gift or souvenir.

Celebrating the most beautiful regions of Britain